Blessing Book

"Twinkle" Marie Porter-Manning

Matrika Press

Blessing Book
Copyright © "Twinkle" Marie Porter-Manning
October 2019

All Rights Reserved
including the right of reproduction,
copying, or storage in any form
or means, including electronic,
In Whole or Part,
without prior written

permission of the author.

ISBN: 978-1-946088-16-1

1.Women's Spirituality 2.Women's Ritual 3.Ceremonies
4.Celebration 5.Bridal Shower 6.Blessingway 7.Title

Matrika Press

Matrika Press
P.O. Box 115
Rockwood, Maine 04478
Editor@MatrikaPress.com

www.MatrikaPress.com

Dedication

Gretchen Ohmann
You have been a source of inspiration from the moment
we met. I deeply appreciate your partnership on so many
programs that serve women's spirituality.
I deeply appreciate our friendship.
I deeply appreciate you.

*To the women who wrote blessings
in my very first handmade Blessing Book:*
Carmen Lohn, Carrie Mancini, Shannon Spaulding,
Morgan Longden, Karissa Spaulding, Josie Libby,
Zoey Spaulding, Sandra Porter,
Audrey Booker, Grace Booker,
Laura Duffy, Autumn Duffy, Willa Duffy,
Kristin Gagnon, Trudy Richmond, Tammy George,
Andrea McCannell, Darcy Rollins, Emily Sprecher,
Heather Sinclair, Grace Sinclair.

*To the beloved Matriarchs of my Women's Circles for your
abiding love, support of and witness to my journey:*
Margaret Stewart, Bozena Smith and Suzanne Foley

I treasure each of you!

Introduction

This book is designed to be included as part of ceremonies honoring women during the milestones and thresholds of their lives. Such gatherings and occasions can include: *Bridal showers, Baby showers, School and College Graduations, Career and Personal Achievements, Retirement Parties, as well as included in rituals for Blessingways, beginning and ending Feminine Moon-cycles, Croning of wise women and other women-honoring ceremonies.*

Blessing Books can be given during times of joy as well as in times of sorrow. Truly whenever a circle of women gather in community to celebrate or support a woman, a Blessing Book can enhance the occasion by providing a cherished gift and beautiful memento to the woman.

How to Use this Blessing Book:

Whether you are in a group gathering, or pass the book from person to person over a period of time, have each one select a word that is meaningful to them. Place the word at the top of selected page. Use the content space provided to describe the significance of this word and/or how the woman being honored may incorporate it into her journey. Be sure to write your name in the designated space at the bottom of the page so she knows this message is from you!

This Blessing Book can also be a personal collection of wisdom words and insights, filled in by a solitary woman as she explores her own thoughts, intuitions, dreams, myths, cycles, spirituality, mind's reasonings and heart's desires.

Wherever you are on your journey, may this Blessing Book serve you well.

For more resources and rituals to accompany this book, including Blessing Stones, visit: MatrikaPress.com/Blessing-Books

This Blessing Book belongs to:

_____

Occasion:

_____

Date:

_____

Table of Contents

1. _____
2. _____
3. _____
4. _____
5. _____
6. _____
7. _____
8. _____
9. _____
10. _____
11. _____
12. _____
13. _____

14. _____
15. _____
16. _____
17. _____
18. _____
19. _____
20. _____
21. _____
22. _____
23. _____
24. _____
25. _____
26. _____
27. _____
28. _____
29. _____
30. _____
31. _____
32. _____
33. _____

34. _____
35. _____
36. _____
37. _____
38. _____
39. _____
40. _____
41. _____
42. _____
43. _____
44. _____
45. _____

Reflections
About the Publisher
About the Author
Other Works by this Author
Coming Soon
Other Books by Matrika Press
Featured Titles
Resources

Written by: _____

Written by: _____

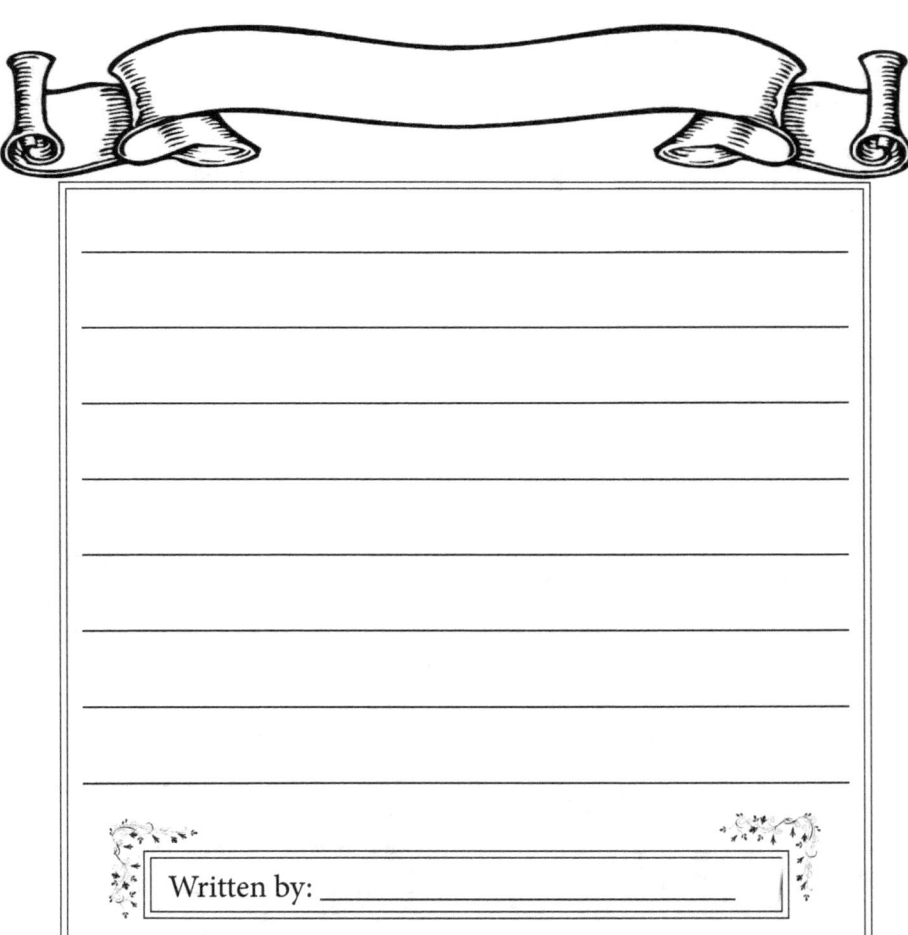

Written by: _____

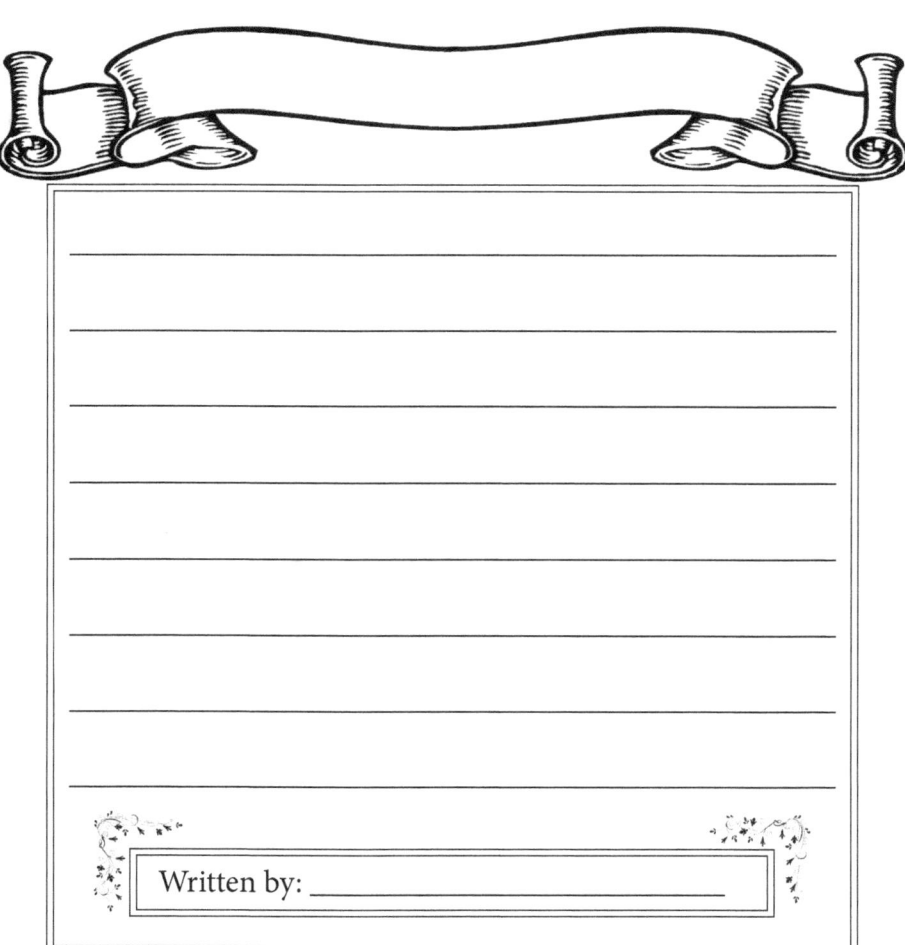

Written by: _____

Written by: _____

Written by: _____

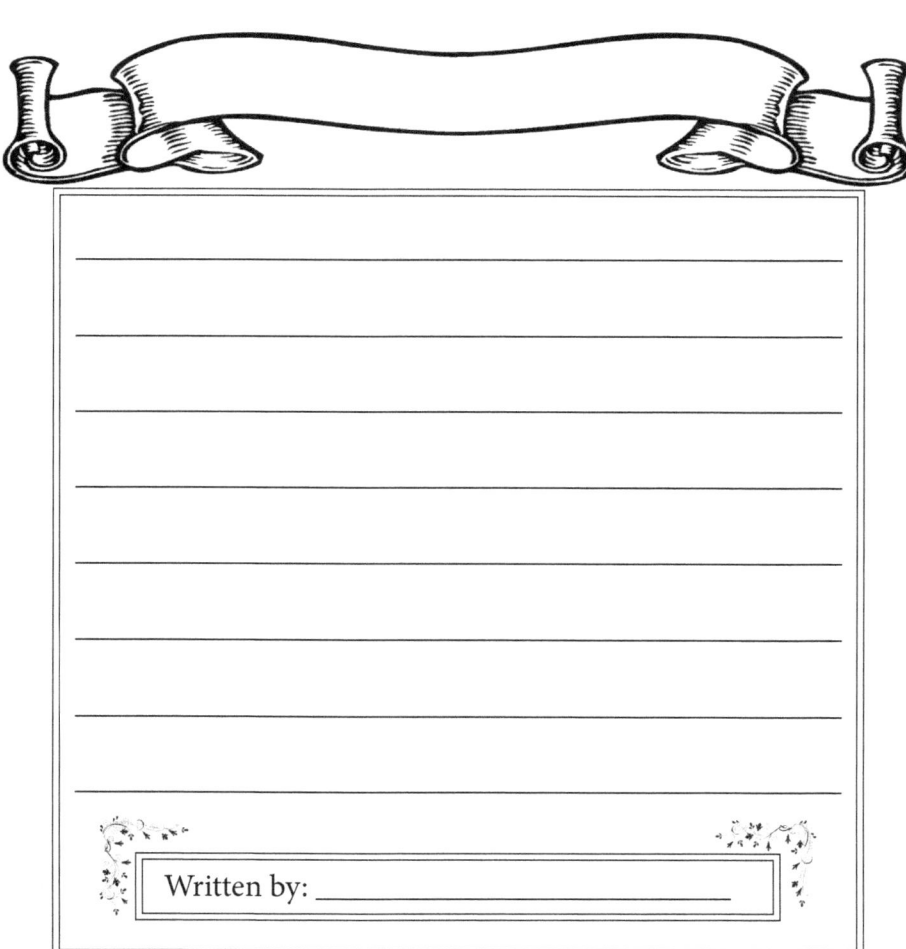

Written by: _____

Written by: _____

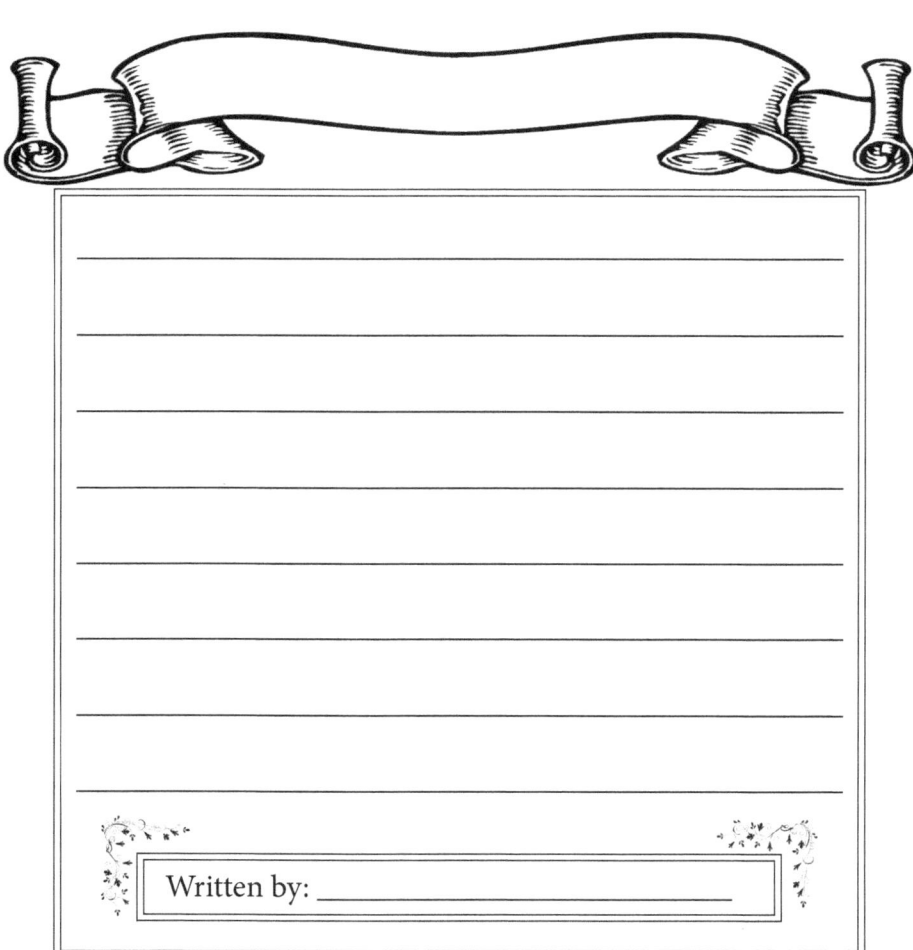

Written by: _____

Written by: _____

Written by: _____

Written by: _____

Written by: _____

Written by: _____

Written by: _____

Written by: _____

Written by: _____

Written by: _____

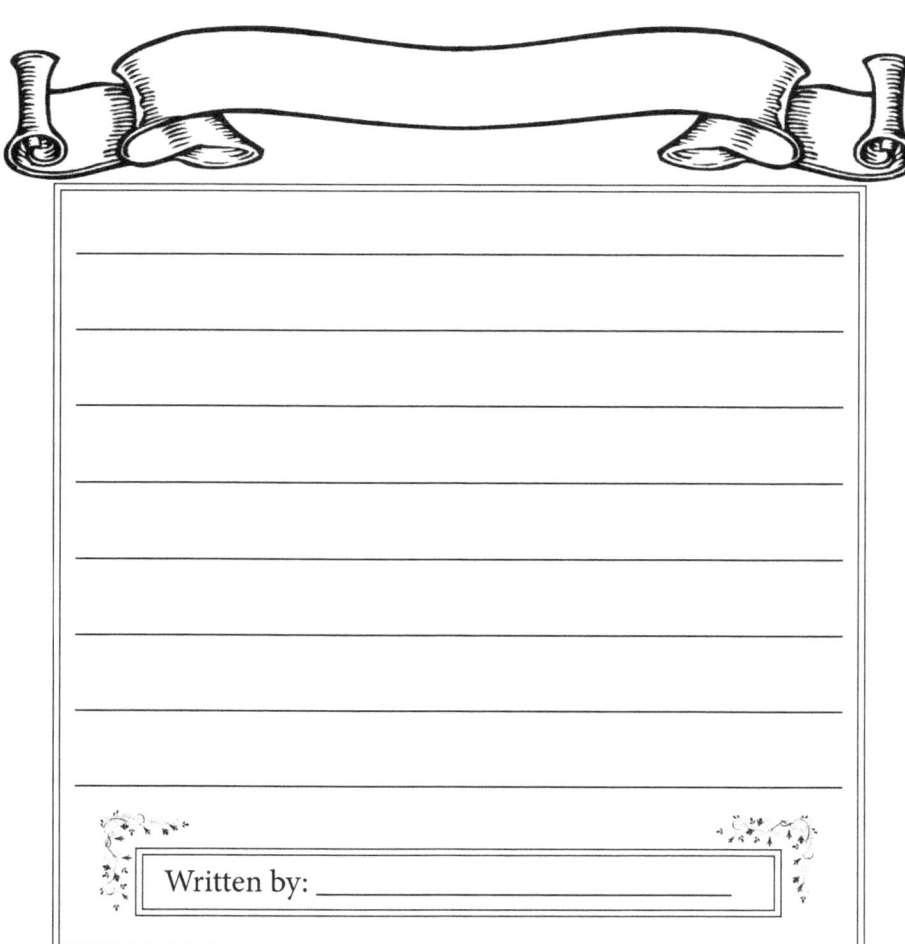

Written by: _____

Reflections

About the Publisher

Matrika Press is an independent publishing house dedicated to publishing works in alignment with liberal religious Values and Principles. Its fiscal sponsor is Unitarian Universalist Women and Religion, a 501c3 organization.

Matrika Press publishes anthologies, memoirs, poetry, prayer and ritual manuscripts, and other books to bring meaning and transformation to the world. A primary goal of Matrika Press is to publish stories and works that would otherwise remain untold. We also resurrect out-of-print manuscripts to ensure our historical works remain accessible.

Matrika Press titles are automatically made available to tens of thousands of retailers, libraries, schools, and other distribution and fulfillment partners, including Amazon, Barnes & Noble, Chapters/Indigo (Canada), and other well-known book retailers and wholesalers across North America, and in the United Kingdom, Europe, Australia and New Zealand and other Global partners.

For more information, visit:

www.MatrikaPress.com

About the Author

Rev. Dr. "Twinkle" Marie Porter-Manning is a skilled ritualist and liturgist who has been leading workshops and seminars in the secular and spiritual worlds for more than two decades. She is the Co-convener for the *Unitarian Universalist Women and Religion* (UUWR.org) organization where she is active in developing and leading programs that nourish women's spirituality. She was the midwife to the *Women's Goddess Covenant Circle* at First Parish in Concord, MA, facilitator of *Sacred Soul Sisters* in California, is the visionary of *Minerva Circles* online gatherings and hosts in-person women spiritual leaders gatherings. She recently published *The Circle Model of Shared Leadership* by Elizabeth Fisher (author of the *Rise Up and Call Her Name* curriculum), the content of which she and her UUWR co-convener Gretchen Ohmann use in teaching collaborative leadership workshops and retreats.

Twinkle is an interfaith minister serving regularly as pulpit resource and consultant for congregations and spiritual groups. She is the *UU Church of the Larger Fellowship*'s *Affiliate Community Minister for Women's Spirituality* and a member of the *UU Society for Community Ministries*. Active in the *International Metaphysical Ministries*, her unique ministry is embraced alongside such wonderful ministries and legacies as that of the amazing Rev. Dr. Della Reese-Lett!

She has published and edited many works, including the *Women of Spirit* anthology series, *Intentional Visualization*, *Be Like the Trees*, *Restore Us to Memory*, and the *Pulpit of Peace* collection. Upcoming works include the *Sophia* anthologies series, *Anam Ċara and The Divine Echo,* and *Möbius Living as Way of Building The Beloved Community and Healing the Loneliness that Exists in the World.*

Her rituals, writings and poetry have been included internationally in all manner of worship services and publications. Her community ministry, affectionately known as *Twinkle's Place*, is approved as a UUA-related organization for Congregational Life for which she currently has two locations in Maine, USA where she hosts a variety of retreats and spiritual programs.

www.MatrikaPress.com/twinkle-marie-manning
www.TwinklesPlace.org

Other Works by this Author

www.MatrikaPress.com/women-of-spirit

Women of Spirit, Exploring Sacred Paths of Wisdom Keepers is a compilation of women sojourners, sages, mystics, witches, shaman, medicine women, ministers, philosophers, therapists, life coaches, yogis, and more.
Their journeys.
Their stories.
Their teachings and practices.
Essays, Poetry, Art, Rituals and Prayers.
This anthology is full of useful tools and powerful messages for everyone who is on a spiritual journey to embrace and enjoy. Beloved Contributors include:
- Anna Huckabee Tull
- Bernadette Rombough
- Deb Elbaum • Deborah Diamond
- Debra Wilson Guttas • Grace Ventura
- Janeen Barnett • JoAnne Bassett
- Judy Ann Foster • Julie Matheson
- Kate Early • Kate Kavanagh
- Katherine Glass • Kris Oster
- Lea M. Hill • Meghan Gilroy
- Morwen Two Feathers • Rustie MacDonald
- Shamanaca • Sharon Hinckley
- Shawna Allard • Shiloh Sophia
- Susan Feathers • Tiffany Cano
- Tory Londergan
- "Twinkle" Marie Porter-Manning
- Tziporah Kingsbury • Valerie Sorrentino

Pulpit of Peace: *Inspirational Quotes from a Prophetic Ministry*

This book features excerpts from Rev. Dr. "Twinkle" Marie Porter-Manning's sermons, as well as glimpses of her poetry, meditations, rituals and reflections. Common themes of her ministry and writings found in this book include:
- Building The Beloved Community;
- Möbius Life;
- Explorations of Divinity;
- Living Life as a Prayer.

Pulpit of Peace is part of the *a Pocketful Book Series*.

Be Like the Trees *(a Sermon in My Pocket)* speaks candidly about tragedy, grief, and challenges faced in daily life. Rev. Dr. "Twinkle" Marie Porter-Manning's words weave together a beautiful collage of insights and inspirations as she directs us towards the interconnectedness and magic of our human existence.

Coming Soon to the "a Sermon in My Pocket" series:

Restore Us to Memory explores remembering (and reclaiming) who we are and offers encouragement to live our lives in such a way that we will be remembered how, and as who, we want to be remembered as.

Anam Ċara and The Divine Echo centers a mystical aspect of belonging, and practical ways to demonstrate such belonging in our lives.

She Stood There is a poem that has been read during blessingways and memorials, as well as for quiet contemplation and meditation. For three decades it has touched hearts and minds as individuals reflect on decisions made when life presents a crossroads.

This is a single poem arranged in a pocket-size book (4×6). Originally penned by the author when she was 17 years old, this poem is about transition, change and choices.

She Stood There is part of the *a Pocketful Book Series..*

Intentional Visualization examines such questions as: Is it true that what we think about comes about? Can we, do we, create our own realities? If we do create our own realities, how do we do so? Ideal for newcomers to law of attraction and metaphysical theologies.

This thesis turned book explores the inter-connection between our thoughts and our life's experiences. Throughout the ages, and certainly in the past several generations, multiple teachers have expressed conviction that there are techniques that will help us create positive outcomes in our lives and for our world, indeed that we can create anything we truly want.

Coming Soon...

Möbius Living *as Way of Building The Beloved Community and Healing the Loneliness that Exists in the World*
In its holistic shaping of The Beloved Community, Möbius Living teaches us to be vigilant about what we are nurturing from the inside out, and the outside in.

www.MatrikaPress.com/twinkle-marie-manning

Other Books by Matrika Press

www.MatrikaPress.com

Featured Titles

The Circle Model of Shared Leadership by Elizabeth Fisher is a concrete group facilitation process that balances achieving tasks with emotional bonding. By using this book you will:
- Learn ways to bring a collection of individuals together, in a committee, board, or activist project, uniting each one's efforts which are equally valued.
- Develop skills critical to honing participatory decision-making and supporting the soul of the group, which must be kept strong if the group is to accomplish its goals.
- Discover important principles, practices and tools that support effective collaboration within and among all the levels of organizations.

www.MatrikaPress.com/the-circle-model

Sue Roy Humphries' historic aggregation work featuring behind-the-scenes documentation of sci-fi and horror classics in theatrical make-up effects has been all but hidden from the world for decades. Originally published in 1980, **Making a Monster** has been long out of print.

Matrika Press is delighted to revive this manuscript on its 40th Anniversary in response to those seeking a comprehensive montage of this highly creative aspect of filmmaking.

Making a Monster reveals the artistic secrets of your favorite vintage fantasy films. This book is filled with detailed accounts of the early era of makeup processes and ingenious solutions to the challenges of pre-CGI Visual FX.

While the manuscript reveals the trade and techniques of transforming some of Hollywood's most beautiful and beloved icons into infamous villains and fantastical creatures, its content also lends a lens unto the human psyche, including that of choosing what to believe in. Said another way, choosing One's Faith.

www.MatrikaPress.com/making-a-monster

The Sophia Anthology Series

In the Spirit of Sophia Magazine, The Journal of Women and Religion, which was published by the Central Midwest District Women and Religion chapter from 1994 through 2004, UUWR is partnering with Matrika Press to create: The Sophia Anthology Series where UU Women's stories and wisdom may be shared.

Submissions may include:
- essays, poetry, meditations, rituals
- customs, songs, chants, art
- personal stories
- experiences on your journey
- lessons you wish to share
- advice you wish to give
- myths (retold or created by you)
- the beauty of nature
- relationship to the divine
- how you honor your truth

UU Poets Series
Seasoned and emerging poets of all genres
are invited to participate in this series.

www.MatrikaPress.com/UU-Poets-Society

Resources

Unitarian Universalist
Women and Religion

Matrika Press and UU Women and Religion leaders are honored to be part of the team of Unitarian Universalist Women who are curating the Heresies Special Collection at Meadville Lombard.

To find out how to help safeguard and celebrate the history of the women who have strengthened and grown Unitarianism, Universalism, and Unitarian Universalism, visit:

www.UUWR.org
www.meadville.edu/donate/heresies/

UU Women Special Collection
MEADVILLE LOMBARD

Empowering Women TV Live Studio Audience Signature Events
EmpoweringWomenTV.org   TVforYourSoul.org

UU Women's Heart TV Series
UUWomensHeart.org

Join Us in Person!

JOIN US ON FACEBOOK!

CLF UU Women's Spirituality Group
Rev. "Twinkle" Marie Manning, *Affiliate Community Minister*

www.MatrikaPress.com

www.ingramcontent.com/pod-product-compliance
Lightning Source LLC
Chambersburg PA
CBHW080027130526
44591CB00037B/2705